Published by
Sparkling Observationalist
sparklingobservationalist.com
thatkatharine.com

©2019 Sparkling Observationalist, Katharine!
All rights reserved.
02 25 19 4 3 2 1

No part of this book may be performed or reproduced in any form without written permission from the author and publisher, except in the context of reviews.

This is a work of fiction. Names, characters, businesses, places, events, locales, and incidents are either the products of the author's imagination or used in a fictitious manner. Any resemblance to actual persons, living or dead, or actual events is purely coincidental.

ISBN: 978-0-9919031-4-6

Miller, Katharine, 1979–
Defying conventions / Katharine Miller.

To everyone who's ever lived, worked, and played in Orlando.

About Defying Conventions

Mermaids in the hot tub, superheroes at the breakfast buffet, ninjas in the tiki lounge — it's just another average weekend at the Belle Royale Palm Vista Plaza Conference Resort and Suites in Orlando, Florida. The hotel is bustling with tacky tourists, wacky cosplayers, and hacky entertainers dealing with misunderstandings, magical mishaps, and mistaken identities. Nothing is what you expect here and everybody's defying conventions.

Defying Conventions is a series of comic stage vignettes all set in the fictional Belle Royale Palm Vista Plaza Conference Resort and Suites of Orlando. Taking place over the course of one summer day, family secrets are spilled during breakfast, a conman puts his heist in jeopardy, cosplayers are subjected to witchcraft, a hypnotist wreaks havoc on ordinary tourists, and two strangers bond over "The Girl From Ipanema."

Ten 10-minute comedies, one hotel, and an assortment of colourful characters.

SCENES

THE FRONT DESK   11
two characters (1F,1M)
In *The Front Desk*, senior tourist-cum-receptionist Stella impresses hotel manager Van with her deft abilities to field odd queries and requests from hotel guests.

FAMILY REUNION   16
three characters (3F)
Family Reunion brings mother Janet together with her two adult daughters Linda and Carla for reminiscences and surprising reveals that challenge the family dynamic.

ESCAPE ROOM   26
three characters (1F, 2M)
Ward and Theresa, a visiting couple from Ohio are stuck in *Escape Room*, hoping that a session with the slick-and-sleazy Eddie, the in-house hotel hypnotist can help.

GOING DOWN   37
six characters (2F, 1M, 3X)
The elevator and a plot to foil a tech billionaire are *Going Down* as Derek struggles to play his role in the big heist.

ATTRACTIONS   43
three characters (2F, 1M)
Tyffyni maintains her professionalism at the hotel information desk in *Attractions* as tourists Priscilla-Grace and Barry get into a dust-up while making plans.

CURSE OF THE KIGURUMI   53
three characters (3X)
In *Curse of the Kigurumi*, three cosplayers return from a convention after

one of their friends has an enchanted encounter with a witch. Can they break the spell or will he be a sock monkey forever?

TOURIST TRAPPED   63
one character, three extras (1F, 3X)
Agnes is a *Tourist Trapped*, stuck entertaining hotel guests by playing piano in cocktail lounges and lamenting the realities of living near the happiest place on Earth.

NO CONTEXT   67
three characters (3M)
There is *No Context* when Mark recognizes Ben from... a popular Internet meme?

SOUVENIRS   74
three characters (2F, 1M)
Souvenirs aren't all that Beverly and Keith are trying to escape with, and Hannah, the hotel's detective is determined to find out why.

DESCONHECIDO   82
two characters (1F, 1M)
Desconhecido finds Linda and Derek in the hotel lounge after a long day dealing with the fall out of their earlier experiences. An unlikely romance blossoms over cocktails and bossa nova.

THE FRONT DESK

Calls about the hotel and situations involving guests are managed.

<u>CAST</u>:
STELLA - (60s+) dressed in hotel receptionist business wear, no name tag
VAN - (40s) hotel manager in tailored suit with shiny hotel name tag

SETTING: *The reception desk in the lobby at the Belle Royale Palm Vista Plaza Conference Resort and Suites of Orlando*

STELLA stands behind the reception desk, typing on the computer. The phone rings.

STELLA: Belle Royale Palm Vista Plaza Conference Resort and Suites of Orlando, how can I help you? I'm sorry, we're booked for the next two weeks. We are a popular destination for conventions and their guests at this time of year. You might try our sister property in Lake Buena Vista, which is actually closer to some of the area's popular theme parks. Yes, it's the Belle Royale Palm Vista Plaza Resort and Spa. I cannot connect you to them directly, ma'am, but their information is on our website. Mm-hmm, that's correct. Good luck and have a pleasant day!
 Front desk, how can I be of service this morning? Nobody likes a lumpy pillow, sir. We do have a pillow menu with a full range of material and support to maximize your comfort and enhance your sleep quality. If you'll check your desk, you'll see a printed copy — it's not there? I will send our pillow steward up to assist you shortly. No problem.
 Front desk, what can I do for you? The hypnotist? Yes, he is on-site this morning. Oh. That is unfortunate. No, of course, no one should have to walk around like that. I will dispatch the hypnotist to your room for a consultation. It should be about fifteen minutes, okay? Perfect.
 Belle Royale Palm Vista Plaza Conference Resort and Suites of Orlando, how can I help you? We are hosting several conventions and conferences here this weekend. Our conference centre is booked for Innovology, National Curators Association, the Central Florida

Faeriefest, and Enthusapalooza. Orlando Sleuthfest? No, that's a mystery to me.

Good morning, you've reached the front desk — we have turn down service, but not tuck-in service. Well, yes, we do have staff to read bedtime stories, as part of our babysitting service for children ages nine and under. No, it doesn't matter if you feel young at heart. I will pass your request onto management. Mm-hmm.

Good morning, front desk — no, ma'am, we have not been invaded by aliens. Many of our guests are attending Ultracon, the big science-fiction convention. Yes, those are people in costumes. Yes, ma'am, it does take real dedication to wear masks in this heat. Yes, we'll post notices encouraging them to stay hydrated.

You've reached Belle Royale Palm Vista Plaza Conference Resort and Suites of Orlando, how may I help you? You can find all of the information about our facilities and amenities on the hotel website. Of course, I can describe them for you, if you prefer. Our resort features recently refurbished guest rooms and suites with plush-top comfort mattresses and bamboo bedding. The bathrooms are stocked with organic spa-quality toiletries — I'm sorry, sir, are you okay? You're breathing heavily and... oh! *Ick!*

Front desk, how may I — you found a hair on your pillow this morning that wasn't yours? And you're completely bald? I'll send the hotel detective to investigate the matter, ma'am.

Hello, Belle Royale Palm Vista Plaza Conference Resort and Suites of Orlando — I'm sorry, we do not have a water park onsite. You want the Belle Royale Palm Vista Plaza Family Resort and Indoor Water Park. Mm-hmm, you're welcome.

Front desk — Fox News is only part of the hotel's pay-per-view entertainment package. No, we can't make an exception for you, sir. Please don't set the curtains on fire. I'm sorry you are dissatisfied with your in-room entertainment options and I will forward your concerns to management. That kind of language is unnecessary, sir. Okay, please hold.

Front desk — you saw mermaids in the hot tub? Please hold. Front desk — the soaps are complimentary, the towels are not. Front desk —

all of our rooms are non-smoking. Oh, your room is smoking?! Maintenance is on their way. Front desk — please hold. Front desk — just a moment, please.

STELLA sets down the phone receiver and takes a moment to catch her breath. VAN approaches the desk.

VAN: What are you doing?

STELLA: Oh, sorry, the phones have been going nonstop this morning. I've dispatched the pillow steward to room 2201, the hypnotist to 835, and the hotel detective to sort out a hairy situation in suite 428. Maintenance is checking out a report of smoke in room 687.

VAN: Thank you. That was beyond the call of duty, especially given the fact that you don't work here.

STELLA: Neither does anyone else, it seems! This desk has been unmanned for hours.

VAN: My apologies. We are a bit understaffed this morning. Do you need something, ma'am?

STELLA: A job.

VAN: A job?

STELLA: Yes, I came here to inquire about applying for a position. I waited for twenty minutes and no one showed up.

VAN: So you took it upon yourself to answer our phones?

STELLA: Yes.

VAN: Where did you get our hotel uniform?

STELLA: You know what they say, dress for the job you want.

VAN: You want to work as a hotel receptionist?

STELLA: Why not? You don't need a fancy degree to stand at a desk and answer questions and telephones. It's an opportunity to meet different kinds of people and make sure their vacations go as smoothly as possible. Doing all that in a beautiful setting like this — what could be better for a woman my age?

VAN: We're not hiring at the moment, ma'am.

STELLA: You said yourself the hotel is understaffed. You should fire whoever was supposed to be here and bring me in.

VAN: We're looking into that. Listen, why don't you go pay a visit to the Belle Royale Palm Vista Corporate Retreat and Golf Spa? I believe they're holding a career fair this afternoon.

STELLA: Thank you. I'll do that. Just one thing.

VAN: Yes?

STELLA: Could I trouble you for a referral?

VAN: You want me to recommend you for a job?

STELLA: If you wouldn't mind. I have been answering telephones for the better part of two hours here. I believe I've demonstrated competence that would rival your most skilled receptionist.

VAN: That may be so, but—

STELLA pulls out a large stack of comment cards.

STELLA: Just look at these guest comment cards.

VAN: These are comments for you?

STELLA: And all glowing reviews of my service, unprompted I'll have you know.

VAN thumbs through the stack of comment cards.

VAN: I'll admit, this is impressive, ma'am.

STELLA: Yes, I thought so, too, sir.

VAN: *(pulls a business card from his coat pocket)* Alright — here's my card. Just have HR contact me and I'll tell them you've been a big help today.

STELLA: Thank you, sir!

STELLA steps out from behind desk with large travel bag and puts on a floppy hat and sunglasses.

STELLA: I can't wait to move to this city! It's so clean and everyone is so friendly. Hope to meet you again soon, Mr. Van. Have a pleasant day!

STELLA exits. VAN steps behind the desk and dials the phone.

VAN: Hello, Dr. Feinman? I just met the woman I'm going to marry.

END OF SCENE. BLACK OUT.

FAMILY REUNION

A mother has breakfast with her two adult daughters while on vacation.

CAST:
JANET - mother (70s), gentle bordering on timid, submissive
CARLA - older daughter (late 40s), bitchy and judgmental in a restrained manner, overly concerned with strangers' perceptions
LINDA - younger daughter (early 40s/late 30s) acerbic, sarcastic, determined to be kind and upbeat

SETTING: The dining room at the Belle Royale Palm Vista Plaza Conference Resort and Suites of Orlando

JANET and LINDA carry breakfast trays to a small two-top table with four chairs crowded around it and sit down.

LINDA: Have you thought about what you want to do today? You want to go to one of the parks? Maybe hit the Orlando outlet malls?

JANET: Let's discuss it with your sister when she gets here.

LINDA: If your hip's bothering you, we could rent one of those scooters.

JANET: We'll see.

LINDA: Okay. *(pokes at the food on her plate)* I know we live in the future, but 3D printed pancakes and scrambled egg patties have to be some of the worst "innovations" yet. Why is the future so determined to put us off of enjoying food?

JANET: Oh, are they not good? You want to get something else?

LINDA: It's fine, Mom. See, with the sausage and egg patties, it looks like a hidden Mickey Mouse.

JANET: Aw, that's cute!

LINDA: Where's Carla and Jenny? We're all eating together, right?

JANET: Oh, I got a text from her while we were in line for food.

JANET gets phone from purse, puts on glasses to find the text and read it.

JANET: *(reading texts from CARLA)* She said, "Are y'all up yet?" And I replied that we were already in the breakfast line. Then she said "What part of 'come to my room first so we can go to breakfast together' don't you understand?"

LINDA: Seriously?

JANET: Well, maybe we ought to go to her room to get her.

LINDA: Nope. We discussed this last night. She agreed to meet us here.

JANET: I'd hate for our day to be spoiled over this. Let's go on up.

LINDA: No. You've already got your breakfast.

JANET: She's upset that we didn't stay at the place she chose.

LINDA: I looked up the motel she chose online. It's cheaper, yes. But it has bedbugs and it's in the middle of nowhere. We'd have been stuck driving everywhere and spent the motel savings on parking at the theme parks. Not to mention, we'd have wasted too much time sitting in traffic and getting lost on the way back, none of which has ever been much fun when we've come here before. This hotel is clean, it has breakfast and a shuttle and a pool. It's conveniently located near a clearly-marked exit off the Interstate, not down a gravel road halfway to Yeehaw Junction.

JANET: *(eager to change the subject)* Look at all these families in matching t-shirts. Should we have matching shirts so people know we're family?

LINDA: Carla gets embarrassed if we *accidentally* wear the same colour.

CARLA stomps up to the table and stands right next to JANET.

CARLA: *(scoffs)* Uh, y'all needed to come get me. I was waiting up there for twenty minutes.

JANET: It's my fault. My hip was bothering me this morning.

CARLA: Well, you need to stay in my room tonight.

JANET: We'll see.

LINDA: Where's Jenny?

CARLA: She slept late and now she's got to do her hair. She won't be down 'til we're done.

LINDA: Ah, teenagers! She's going to miss her chance to eat like it's 2099. *(holds up rubbery pancake)*

CARLA just shakes her head in disgust. She sits in the chair closest to JANET.

CARLA: Why are there so many people in costumes here? It ain't Halloween.

LINDA: There's a comic book convention in town.

CARLA: So they're all dressed as superheroes?

LINDA: Most of them. It's a big thing now.

CARLA: That's stupid.

JANET: It's fun to see all these dressed up people. We don't even need to go to the parks. Aww, look, there's the princess sisters from that movie. Just like y'all are my princess sisters.

CARLA: *(scoffs)* Well, they ain't superheroes.

LINDA: We should decide if we're going, though, if we want to catch the shuttle bus.

JANET: I don't know if I'm up for the heat and the lines in the parks, but you girls can go ahead if you want.

LINDA: I'm here for *you*, Mom. If you don't want to go anywhere, we'll sit by the pool and let boys bring us fruity umbrella drinks.

JANET: We could just sit in the room as long as I'm spending quality time with my girls.

CARLA: Jenny wants me to drive her over to SeaWorld later.

LINDA rolls her eyes.

JANET: Are you gonna eat anything before you go, Carla? You want my yogurt?

CARLA: You know I don't eat in the morning. Did you take your pills yet?

JANET: Yes'm.

LINDA: What pills?

JANET: My little-old-lady pills that keep me from dying.

LINDA: Are you in danger of dying?

JANET: Not right now.

CARLA: Can y'all not talk about dying?

LINDA: I'm just curious about our mother's health. Sorry.

JANET: They found a little bit of cancer in my bosom a while ago but we did some radiation and now I just take some pills.

LINDA: You've had cancer? And you didn't think to mention it?!

CARLA: Shhh!

JANET: I didn't tell you? Well, I didn't want to burden you. You're all grown up and have your own life. You don't want to be with your old, sick mother.

CARLA: *Mama—*

LINDA: Don't judge us based on how we were as bratty teenagers. All teenage girls hate their mothers.

CARLA: Mine doesn't. She wrote in her diary that I'm her best friend.

LINDA: Jenny lets you read her diary?

CARLA: She *knows* I read it.

JANET: I remember, Carla, you used to read your diary out loud to me. I don't know why you thought your mama needed to know you were kissing so many boys.

LINDA: Bragging.

CARLA: I didn't talk about kissing boys.

JANET: I remember the kissing.

LINDA: Remember when you made out with the guy from the ice machine at that Holiday Inn in Pensacola?

CARLA: No.

LINDA: C'mon! You wrote in your diary how you met some guy while getting ice for Mom's morning Coca-Cola. He told you that he was the drummer for Pablo Cruise and offered you tickets to their show that night. He said you were "so fine"— which was the highest compliment back in the day. Mom wouldn't let you go to the concert, but you did sneak out after we were asleep to go make out with the guy in the parking lot behind the tour bus for — what did you say it was — twenty-three minutes. Hey, whatever happened to Pablo Cruise? Did you guys keep in touch?

CARLA: Don't talk about this stuff around my daughter.

LINDA: What? You don't read your diary *to her*? Some best friend!

JANET: Now, girls. Let's not fight. We had such a pleasant supper last night.

LINDA: Oh, right. We're still mad at you for not telling us you were sick.

JANET: I'm better now.

LINDA: Are you just telling us you're better?

CARLA: She's better.

LINDA: How do you know?

CARLA: I was there.

JANET: She moved in with me last year, around Christmas. Are you sure I didn't tell you any of this? She sat with me through all the doctors' appointments and treatments.

LINDA: I'd remember my mother having cancer. I would've come home.

JANET: Well, your sister was with me.

LINDA: That doesn't matter! We're not the same person. We're not interchangeable. What if you'd needed my blood or an organ or something?

CARLA: Shh! People are staring at us.

LINDA: There are three Spider-mans, an 80-year-old Superman, and a fat, hairy middle-aged man dressed as the Little Mermaid. Nobody's looking at us.

JANET: I just wanted us to have a peaceful vacation. Who knows if this could be the last one we have together.

CARLA: Don't say that, Mama.

JANET: I know I made mistakes with you girls when you were little —

LINDA: This isn't about something that happened back in 1985. You *just* had breast cancer and completely shut me out.

JANET: We didn't want to force you to be somewhere you didn't want to be.

LINDA: This again? Not everyone wants to stay in their hometown forever. I moved away. It's not like I abandoned you to shack up with chain-smoking floozy like Daddy did.

JANET: We're together now and that's what's important.

LINDA: Why are we here now? All we're going to do is sit in Carla's room and stare at the Rorschach floral paintings that pass for art in these hotels until it's too late to actually do anything. I guess it's nice to be able to look out at the palm trees while arguing over who made Daddy run off with the redheaded waitress from Steak 'n' Shake. Hey, why don't we go full-on Tennessee Williams — let's shut off the air conditioner and swelter in this white-washed swamp until we spill all of our family secrets or die trying. Ooh — maybe Mom isn't really my mother at all!

CARLA: God! You think you know better'n everybody 'cause you ran away and went to art school. I know you love swooping into town, showing off with your big words and your Yankee accent, making sure we all see how smart you are. If we had told you about Mama, you'd've showed up and brought her a bunch of hippie cancer cookbooks she ain't gonna use and you'd've complained about how dumb and fat everybody is and picked on us for watching reality TV instead of some boring English thing ain't no one heard of but you. Mama was sick and didn't need your high horse attitude.

LINDA: So...because I'm pretentious, I don't deserve to be with you during life-or-death situations? Some family.

JANET: This is where we used to come for vacations when you were young. I guess I thought it would be nice to have one more family vacation here. We are family, like it or not. You girls only get one mama — and I am both y'all's mama.

The women sit in silence for a moment. CARLA pulls out her phone to text as

JANET and LINDA keep their respective emotions at bay.

LINDA: *(attempting to diffuse the tension)* I guess this isn't the worst breakfast we've ever had on vacation. Remember Ocala? When Daddy brought Darlene to the Waffle House?

CARLA: Ugh. I wish he'd've died then.

LINDA: They found out we were in town and came over to gloat about how they'd bought a horse farm nearby and said me and Carla were welcome to go riding with 'em anytime we wanted.

CARLA: That witch knew we weren't gonna ride no horses.

JANET: Was that when we went to Silver Springs and did the glass bottom boat? Oh, I liked that place. So calm and restful.

CARLA's phone buzzes with a text.

CARLA: Shit. Jenny says she met a boy by the pool. He invited her to go play putt-putt.

LINDA: Like mother, like daughter.

JANET: Let her go if she wants. She can sit with her old, dying grandmama any time.

CARLA: I ain't gonna let her go off with no boy.

LINDA: Like mother, like daughter.

CARLA gets up and leaves.

JANET: We best go with her.

LINDA helps JANET get out of her chair and they start towards the exit.

LINDA: You go on ahead. If we're going to stay in the room, we're going to need some ice.

JANET: Alright then. Don't *you* talk to any strange boys at the ice machine now, y'hear.

LINDA: Yes'm.

LINDA watches JANET exit the breakfast room. LINDA returns to the table, slumps into her chair and stares into the distance as tears well up.

END OF SCENE. BLACKOUT.

ESCAPE ROOM

A vacationing couple struggle with the husband's revelation. Desperate to keep this from ruining the trip, the wife brings in the hotel hypnotist.

CAST:
WARD - husband (40s), dressed in pajamas
THERESA - wife (40s), dressed for a day at the theme parks (shorts, Disney-themed tank top or t-shirt, hip/fanny pack)
EDDIE - brash hypnotist (50s), wearing a sparkly/sequin blazer over a polo shirt and khakis, might have a bunch of junk in his pockets from his show — postcards, pocket watch, novelty sunglasses

SETTING: A hotel room in the Belle Royale Palm Vista Plaza Conference Resort and Suites of Orlando

WARD and THERESA sit on the edge of the bed.

WARD: It won't work.

THERESA: It won't hurt to try.

WARD groans.

THERESA: We could've just stayed at the Sandusky Ramada if this is all we were gonna do. Come on! I want to see some sights. I want to seek some thrills.

WARD: I know, I know.

THERESA: I thought you wanted to come to Orlando. You were really excited over the brochures.

WARD: What can I say? I'm a sucker for glossy travel brochures.

THERESA: We've been cooped up in this room for three days, Ward.

WARD: There are pirates in the gazebo, Theresa.

THERESA: *(sighs)* Yes.

WARD: And wizards in the lobby and superheroes at the pool and ninjas in the elevator.

THERESA: What if we covered your eyes? We could use a blindfold or put a bag over your head and you could pretend that everything is normal.

WARD: Why don't you put a bag over your head and I'll turn on the Disney channel and you can pretend you're in Fantasyland?

THERESA starts to respond, but there's a knock at the door.

THERESA: God, I hope this works.

WARD: What kind of hypnotist makes house calls in a hotel at 9:30 in the morning?

THERESA opens the door and EDDIE barges into the room.

EDDIE: Alright, where's the big chicken?

WARD raises his hand.

EDDIE: Huh. I don't remember you from last night. Do I have the right room? Enh, all tourists look alike, I guess. You ready? When I snap my fingers, you will no longer think you are a chicken.

THERESA: No, hold on, we didn't see your show last night. He's not that kind of chicken.

EDDIE: *(to THERESA)* Well, hello there. I would certainly remember seeing you. How're you doing, bright eyes?

THERESA: We're hoping you can help us. My husband here is afraid of costumed characters and refuses to leave the room.

EDDIE: The ol' Masklophobia, huh?

WARD: Yes! You've heard of it?

THERESA sits next to WARD on the bed.

THERESA: We've been together nearly twenty years and this is the first I'm hearing of it.

EDDIE: In my business, you hear it all — every phobia, quirk, kink and peccadillo. You name it, I've heard of it. Masklophobia — how long you had it?

EDDIE paces around the edge of the bed, in front of WARD and THERESA, while digging around in his pockets. When he gets upstage of WARD, he pulls out a pair of novelty sunglasses. EDDIE puts on the sunglasses and hovers behind WARD.

WARD: All my life. It started when my mom took me to the mall Santa and I screamed my head off before she could set me on his lap.

THERESA: Everyone's scared of the mall Santas.

WARD: The same thing happened with the Easter Bunny. Clowns make me clammy. Drag queens make me dizzy. I've fainted at the sight of a funny hat. I couldn't even try out for sports because I was terrified of the team mascots. Don't get me started on Halloween.

EDDIE grasps WARD's shoulder.

EDDIE: And yet you came to Orlando?

WARD turns to see EDDIE wearing the sunglasses and pulling a silly face. WARD shrieks and covers his eyes. As he rocks back and forth in panic, THERESA tries to soothe him.

EDDIE: For a nice Florida vacation, you head to the coast, to Miami, Cocoa Beach, maybe Pensacola. Orlando is strictly Mickey Mouse. You can't go anywhere in this town without seeing some kook in a costume. And in the height of convention season? Forget it! Every Tom, Dick, and Harry Potter's down here with conventions for comic books, movies, I dunno what. It's 100 degrees in the shade and these kids are out there voluntarily wearing chain mail and big foam heads. Nuts!

EDDIE removes the sunglasses and shoves them back into his pocket. He gives WARD a reassuring pat on the back. WARD peeks out through his fingers, sighs, and uncovers his face.

WARD: Why are you here so early in the morning? Don't you perform at night?

EDDIE: Sometimes my audience volunteers relapse into their trances overnight and — after several lengthy discussions with lawyers — the hotel likes to make sure I'm on hand to snap 'em out it.

THERESA: Can you do something about this?

EDDIE: For you, bright eyes, I will make the most concentrated effort.

THERESA: Please, I need to get out of this room.

EDDIE assesses the situation, looking over WARD and THERESA. His attention is drawn to THERESA.

EDDIE: Boy! I just can't get over your eyes. Stunning. Absolutely gorgeous!

THERESA: Thanks?

EDDIE squeezes onto the bed between the couple. He leans into THERESA and gazes deep into her eyes.

EDDIE: Let me look into them a little closer. They're just so mesmerizing — and I should know!

THERESA tries to look away but can't quite resist EDDIE's seductive gaze.

EDDIE: Your eyes twinkle, but when I look deeper, there's something— a sadness... a dormant desire?

THERESA: Hmm.

EDDIE: I can see you're yearning for adventure.

THERESA: Yeah?

EDDIE: You crave excitement and passion!

THERESA: Well—

EDDIE: It feels like forever since you had a good time.

THERESA: Yes!

EDDIE grabs THERESA hands and clutches them passionately.

EDDIE: After twenty years in Toledo, you're finally ready to break free from the shackles of matrimony and find someone who can fulfill your fantasies and make your every wish come true!

THERESA: Yes! Wait, no... *(pulls her hands away from EDDIE)* I just want to ride in the tea cups and meet the Genie from *Aladdin*.

WARD clears his throat. EDDIE turns to WARD.

EDDIE: How long you been here?

WARD: Are you hitting on my wife?

EDDIE: Who's hitting? I'm just being friendly. I'm a naturally friendly guy.

WARD: Naturally.

EDDIE: You're not offended, are you, bright eyes?

THERESA: It's harmless, I suppose.

EDDIE: When was the last time this guy looked at anything beyond the television set?

THERESA: It's been a while, yes, but —

WARD: You're shameless.

EDDIE: I'm no marriage counselor, but you know the old saying "happy wife, happy life"? I've got three monthly alimony payments to prove it, buddy.

THERESA: Ward, darling, I get one week's vacation every year. I want to have fun. I need to have fun. Being stuck in a hotel room with you watching TV is not fun. Wouldn't you like to have fun instead of continuing to let this phobia cripple you?

WARD: *(to EDDIE)* What do you suggest?

EDDIE: We could do a little manipulation of the mind.

EDDIE ushers WARD from the bed and into a chair.

WARD: My mother tried clinical hypnotherapy on me once. It didn't take.

EDDIE: Pffft. Hypnotherapists are the chiropractors of the mind. They claim they'll fix you but it'll take a lot of time — and a whole lotta dough. All you need is a little power of suggestion to modify your behaviour.

WARD: So you can trick me into thinking I'm not scared of costumes?

EDDIE: What's a costume but something somebody puts on to pretend they're someone else? To that end, a uniform could be a costume. How do ya know?

WARD: I never considered that.

EDDIE: See, hypnosis works best when the mind can fixate on one task. The mind responds faster to a specific suggestion than abstract behaviour modification. Instead of saying "You will no longer be terrified of random articles of clothing", we opt for something easier like, "You will now think you're Elvis" or "You will now behave like a chicken". The simpler the suggestion, the more receptive the mind is to the suggestion.

WARD: You're not gonna turn me into a chicken.

EDDIE: Do I look like a magician? I can't turn you into a chicken, with the beak and the feathers. I can only make you think you're a chicken.

THERESA: Wouldn't that be embarrassing in public?

EDDIE: So he clucks a little, pecks at the ground, does a little strut. With everything else going on in this town, you're worried?

WARD: *(to THERESA)* Honey, is that the trade-off you want? You'd rather drag a chicken-man through the theme parks instead of staying in the room with your normal husband?

THERESA: Both options are foul.

EDDIE: Wordplay! Ha! Funny and cute, just like my second wife.

WARD: Turn my wife into a chicken and she won't care if we stay in the room.

THERESA finds her own sunglasses and quickly puts them on as she moves away from the men.

WARD: Look, this phobia is not one of my finer qualities, I'll admit, but you're all making light of it as if I've made a deliberate choice to be petrified of people playing dress up. How was I to know Orlando is the cosplay destination of America? They didn't print that in their fancy pamphlets! You think I like being trapped in here?! I haven't slept since we arrived, I don't know how we'll get home or if I can even look at a pair of sunglasses anymore!

WARD sees THERESA wearing her sunglasses and starts to hyperventilate. EDDIE grabs WARD's shoulders and gently massages them. As EDDIE speaks, WARD begins to calm down.

EDDIE: Hey, relax. We're all on your side, buddy. Take a deep breath. Aren't you feeling a little drowsy? You look tired. Why don't you think about getting some sleep. I bet you'll feel a lot better after a nap. You like kitty cats?

WARD: I love kitty cats. *(yawns)* I wish I were a kitty cat.

EDDIE digs through his pockets and pulls out a folded up postcard of the "hang in there" kitty poster. He unfolds the postcard and shows it to WARD.

EDDIE: Okay, look at this cat. Relax and focus on this kitty cat. Take a deep breath. Don't speak. Don't think. Just listen to me and look at this cute little kitty cat.

WARD responds to EDDIE's hypnotic suggestions.

EDDIE: Your eyes are getting heavy, don't fight it. A little cat nap is just what you need. That's right. You are sound asleep. When you wake up, you will behave like an ordinary house cat. All the stresses of your human world will disappear and you will think and live like a cat. When I clap my hands, you will emerge from your slumber in a fully cat-like state. Here, kitty, kitty!

EDDIE claps his hands and WARD perks up. WARD leans over to sniff EDDIE's hand. He leaps from the chair onto the bed, licks his "paw" and rubs his face. EDDIE crumples up the postcard and waves it around to tease WARD, who focuses on it intently, like a cat. EDDIE tosses the crumpled paper ball across the room and WARD scrambles after it. He bats the ball around the floor and pounces on it.

THERESA: Wow.

EDDIE: Damn, I'm good.

THERESA: Is he really a cat now?

EDDIE: He believes he's a cat.

THERESA: How long will this trance last?

EDDIE: As long as you want, bright eyes.

THERESA: I don't think I've ever seen him so active. It'll be a shame to get him back to normal.

EDDIE: No reason this couldn't be his new normal. Some of my clients tell me they were much happier as chickens.

THERESA giggles as WARD engages in playful cat-like activity.

THERESA: But, Eddie, I don't think this solves my problem.

EDDIE: Sure it does.

WARD continues play as a cat in the background while EDDIE and THERESA discuss their plans.

THERESA: Can I really take him anywhere like this? How do we know he won't still have an adverse reaction to costumes?

EDDIE: You think I turned the big chicken into a scaredy cat?

THERESA: I think he might pounce on Mickey Mouse.

EDDIE: Leave him.

THERESA: Can he be left alone?

EDDIE: Sure! He'll never know the difference. We'll send room service up with some tuna fish. The staff in this joint have seen weirder stuff, believe me.

THERESA: I don't know that I want to go to an amusement park by myself.

EDDIE: Look, my show isn't until later tonight. I could take you around, join you for a spin in the tea cups, introduce you to some real colourful characters. The genie happens to be one of my best friends. We go bowling every Thursday.

THERESA: Oh, well, if it's no trouble...

EDDIE: Spending the day in the company of a beautiful woman is trouble I can handle.

As THERESA goes to grab a tote bag and floppy hat, WARD jumps up on the table to hiss and yowl at EDDIE.

EDDIE: *(hisses back)* You blew it, buddy. Don't be such a pussy next time.

THERESA and EDDIE discuss possible destinations as they exit the room. EDDIE is careful to close the door behind them. WARD scampers over and madly scratches at the door to be let out.

END OF SCENE. BLACK OUT.

GOING DOWN

A plan unfolds in the elevator. Misunderstandings and surprises emerge as the main characters reveal their roles.

<u>CAST</u>:
SUSAN - *a youngish businesswoman in business casual attire, carrying a briefcase*
DEREK - *a rough-looking guy of indeterminate age with greasy hair, leather jacket and loud print shirt*
NATASHA - *a mysterious woman wearing trench coat and sunglasses*
ROCK STAR *with conference badge on lanyard for BizDev Summit*
NINJA *with conference badge on lanyard for BizDev Summit*
GURU *with conference badge on lanyard for BizDev Summit*

SETTING: *Interior of an elevator in the Belle Royale Palm Vista Plaza Conference Resort and Suites of Orlando*

SUSAN enters the elevator. DEREK runs up to the elevator and grabs the doors to keep them from closing on him as he enters. SUSAN nods and smiles politely as DEREK takes his place next to her in elevator.

DEREK: Lots of crazy costumes around here this weekend, eh?

SUSAN: Seems so.

DEREK: I was just stuck behind a family of Stormtroopers in the corridor. Like, a real family with a mum and dad and baby Stormtrooper in the pram. That's not something you see every day, is it?

SUSAN: It isn't.

DEREK: What's the weirdest one you've seen?

SUSAN: Hm. There was an 80-year-old Superman in line at the breakfast buffet moving around like he had a pocket full of kryptonite.

DEREK nods, considers what SUSAN said, and slyly sneaks a peek at the palm of his hand, where there's a code phrase written on it.

DEREK: Sorry, like a what?

SUSAN: He had a pocket full of kryptonite?

DEREK looks at his palm and mouths the phrase. Unable to quite make out the writing, he squints and rubs at the ink. He shrugs and then coolly leans into SUSAN.

DEREK: *(pulls a pen from his breast pocket and passes it to SUSAN)* Take this pen.

SUSAN, puzzled, takes the pen and examines it.

DEREK: The tech mogul Elton Stench is planning to introduce an invasive brain-hacking app at the Innovology conference today. It could potentially destroy free will as we know it. That pen contains a flash drive with a virus that will corrupt the Mind Minder app and prevent Stench from demonstrating it. Your job is to get this to the Crystal Frond ballroom, where our man will be waiting to plug it into Stench's laptop, just before the presentation begins. In the meantime, the rest of our crew will be in his suite to steal the platinum hard drive that holds the original Mind Minder files. Got it?

SUSAN: I think you've mistaken me for someone else.

DEREK: Oh, I thought you were the — no? Ah.

SUSAN: Did you say you're here for Innovology?

DEREK: Uh… Nooooo. I am on my way to the, er, CaperCon. It's an event for fictional con men. I'm, uh, Keyser Soze. I was just getting into character, y'know. If you want, I'll take the pen—

DEREK gestures for the pen. SUSAN starts to pass it back, but pauses.

SUSAN: From *The Usual Suspects*? I don't recall a brain-hacking app as part of the plot.

DEREK: Er, it's from the latest remake. *(scoffs)* You know Hollywood, always remaking things.

SUSAN: Mm-hmm.

Elevator dings. A ROCK STAR, NINJA, and GURU enter and stand in front of SUSAN and DEREK while carrying on a dry exchange about business development. As they speak, DEREK checks his palm to compare their chats against his code phrase.

ROCK STAR: ...thereby incentivizing corporations to insource projects and foster interdepartmental collaboration.

NINJA: The gap analysis shows that rapid insourcing challenges long-term growth opportunities with existing partners.

GURU: The key is to formulate a strategy to implement continuous, vertical integration while strengthening the value chain, which improves core competence and provides a competitive advantage over a corporate infrastructure that relies on outsourcing functions.

Elevator dings. The ROCK STAR, NINJA and GURU exit.

SUSAN: Sounds like there's a lot of cons happening this weekend.

DEREK: *(nervous laugh)* Ha, yes. Lots of cons. Comic cons. Business cons. Long cons, short cons, ex-cons. It's the wrath of cons. *(clears throat)* I've never understood the difference between conferences and conventions. You wouldn't happen to know, would you?

SUSAN: I don't. They all seem to require wearing lanyards and spending hours in confined spaces chatting with insufferable show-offs. You do get more complimentary pens at business conferences. Oh, speaking of, did you want your pen back?

DEREK: Oh, er, I don't suppose you'd be willing to—

SUSAN starts to return the pen to DEREK.
Elevator dings. NATASHA enters. DEREK is forced to shift behind the two women before he can retrieve the pen.

NATASHA: The fox is full of crepes tonight.

No one responds.

NATASHA: *(slightly louder)* The fox is full of crepes tonight.

DEREK looks at his palm again, realizes that must the code phrase. He tries to grab the pen from SUSAN but it's too late.

SUSAN: *(passes the pen to NATASHA)* You know what to do?

NATASHA: Ja. Danke.

SUSAN: De nada.

Elevator dings. NATASHA exits.
SUSAN's mobile phone rings.

SUSAN: *(on phone)* I'm on my way now, Mr. Stench. Everything's all set, sir. See you soon. *(puts phone away, pulls a key card from her briefcase and offers it to DEREK)* Your team will find the hard drive in the safe behind the imitation Rothko painting. The decoy drive is tucked inside the toilet tank. Remove it from the waterproof bag and place it inside the safe. You will have 17 minutes to complete this job, before the virus is triggered on Mr. Stench's presentation laptop. When the job is done, there's a car out front to take the crew to a hideout, where you will wait for further instructions. Got it?

DEREK: You're the —? And his —?

SUSAN: Asking too many questions can be hazardous for a man in your profession. Mind Minder is a dangerous program on a good day, even more so if it fell into the wrong hands. Mr. Stench is too often shaking those wrong hands.

DEREK: Sorry, it's just—

SUSAN: Unexpected? Yes. I didn't get to be the right-hand woman of the most powerful tech magnate without a few tricks up my sleeve.

DEREK: Does Stench know?

SUSAN: Mr. Stench might be a genius, but there's much he does not know.

DEREK and SUSAN stand in silence for a beat as DEREK tries to process.

DEREK: Listen, er, about before, with the mix-up —

SUSAN: Your cover was almost plausible. However, try to keep chit-chat to a minimum on the ride back up?

DEREK: Yes, ma'am. Can I ask, though, what you're planning to do with the hard drive?

SUSAN: It will be destroyed.

DEREK: It's gotta be worth a lot of money, though? Like, there's probably a demand for it on the black market.

SUSAN: The Mind Minder program tracks and logs all brain activity — every fleeting thought and foolhardy scheme, your wildest fantasies and deepest desires. I'm not interested in profiting off the exploitation of private thoughts. What any powerful organization would do with that data is anybody's guess, but it could mean this is the last heist you and your friends ever pull.

DEREK: *(muses to himself over possibilities)* If we collected enough dough, we'd never think about pulling another con. I'm ready to get out of the business anyway. Maybe become a screenwriter or buy a horse farm or something. Hey, I could invent my own app!

Elevator dings.

SUSAN: The fate of free thought is in your hand. What's it gonna be?

DEREK: Jeez, no pressure, huh? *(studies the keycard for a moment)* Okay, alright! Let's free the minds and eliminate that Stench! Ooh, I should write that down.

SUSAN exits the elevator.
DEREK pulls a notebook and pen out of his coat pocket, starts to click the pen top, looks at pen.

DEREK: Shit.

Elevator doors close as DEREK remains inside.

END OF SCENE. BLACKOUT.

ATTRACTIONS

A hotel employee works the information desk and interacts with guests.

<u>CAST</u>:
PRISCILLA-GRACE - (40-ish) chatty, Southern, annoying with good intentions, carrying an oversized tote bag with a large urn inside
BARRY - (50-ish) nebbish-looking yet slimy Southern redneck
TYFFYNI - (20s) hotel employee, doing her best to remain professional

SETTING: *The information desk in the lobby of the Belle Royale Palm Vista Plaza Conference Resort and Suites of Orlando*

TYFFYNI, *bored, stands behind an information desk.*
PRISCILLA-GRACE *enters, pulls a plastic baggie out of her tote bag and sprinkles dust from the baggie into a potted palm located near the entrance. She blows a kiss to the plant and wanders over to the brochure rack near the information desk.*

PRISCILLA-GRACE: *(holds up a couple of brochures)* Which is better — the interactive murder mystery dinner theatre or the interactive pirate ship dinner theatre?

TYFFYNI: I don't know, ma'am.

PRISCILLA-GRACE: No? I thought, this being the information desk, you'd be the expert.

TYFFYNI: My apologies, ma'am. Ironically, this job doesn't give me a lot of time, er, opportunity to scope out the local attractions. Other guests seem to like them both.

PRISCILLA-GRACE: Bless my heart, you live here! Why would you go to these tourist places, especially when you've got all this gorgeous weather. I bet you'd rather be at the beach right now.

TYFFYNI: It's not always gorgeous. We get a lot of rain.

PRISCILLA-GRACE: Did you see that storm out in the ocean right now?

TYFFYNI: Hurricane Jesús?

PRISCILLA-GRACE: Oh, *hay-Zeus*? Ha! I was watching the TV news with the sound off! I do hope he fizzles out fast. I live up in Mobile and I've seen plenty of storms get weak passing over Orlando just to turn back into a big ol' hurricane when it gets into the Gulf. We still got a bunch of blue tarps up after what hit us last year.

TYFFYNI: Sorry to hear that. We hope you have a good vacation anyway.

PRISCILLA-GRACE browses brochures.

PRISCILLA-GRACE: My family used to come down here all the time when I was little. Daddy loved all the roadside attractions and, oh, he worshipped Walt Disney. Mama complained that it took us twice as long to get here because we had to stop at all these tacky little places, but she liked stopping to see the mermaids at Weeki-Wachee more than any of the Magic Kingdom rides. Have you ever been to Weeki-Wachee?

TYFFYNI: I just work here, ma'am.

PRISCILLA-GRACE: If you get a chance, go before they close for good. It's so inspiring to see those girls — what a dream come true that must be! We stopped by there yesterday and it was like no time had passed. It does look a little run down, though, like it could use a fresh coat of paint—

TYFFYNI: Are you waiting for someone, ma'am? I can have them paged for you.

PRISCILLA-GRACE: Oh, no. I'm traveling alone. Well, mostly. See, my Daddy passed on recently and we had decided that I would spread his ashes around all our old vacation spots.

TYFFYNI: I'm sorry for your loss.

PRISCILLA-GRACE: Thank you. It was coming for a while. I guess you can't live on Moon Pies and Co-Cola forever. Anyway, I'm on a mission to let Daddy rest in the places he loved most.

TYFFYNI: You're doing that for your whole vacation?

PRISCILLA-GRACE: Yes'm. That's the idea. I'm not real sure I can get him into the big parks, what with security being nasty since 9/11 and all. I can't imagine they'll look kindly on baggies full of gray dirt.

TYFFYNI: Bags? You don't have an urn?

PRISCILLA-GRACE: When they gave me his remains, it was just this big ol' cardboard box that could fill half a dozen urns and a couple of these palm tree pots. And he wasn't even a very large man. I left the box up in my room and been filling up a bunch of little Ziploc baggies with him for our day trips. Oh, I hope the maids don't throw him out!

TYFFYNI: I'll get a message to housekeeping.

PRISCILLA-GRACE: Would you? Bless you!

TYFFYNI: You should get a special Florida-themed urn for him.

PRISCILLA-GRACE: That's a good idea. Oh! You know what'd be real cute is to have a Florida snow globe made with him!

TYFFYNI: Uh-huh.

PRISCILLA-GRACE: I wonder if there's a place on International Drive that does that?

TYFFYNI: I can look that up for you.

PRISCILLA-GRACE: Aren't you sweet? Thank you.

TYFFYNI starts typing at her computer.
BARRY enters and strides up to the info desk.

BARRY: The Parrotheads leaving from here?

TYFFYNI: They left an hour ago, sir.

BARRY: *(checks his watch)* Ain't they oughta be leaving in five minutes?

TYFFYNI: The only Parrotheads group we have on schedule for today is the "Shakin' Singles' Salty Scavenger Hunt" and they left an hour ago.

BARRY: Goddamn it.

PRISCILLA-GRACE: Did you set your watch when you arrived?

BARRY: It's got a battery.

TYFFYNI: What time zone do you live in, sir?

BARRY: The American one?

PRISCILLA-GRACE: Where are you from?

BARRY: Pensacola. Why's y'all asking? Whassit matter for what I'm doing?

TYFFYNI: Our time zones are different. Pensacola is in the Central time zone. Orlando is in the Eastern time zone.

BARRY: That's dumb. It should be the same time all over the same state.

PRISCILLA-GRACE: It sure is confusing.

BARRY: It wasted me a shitload of money.

PRISCILLA-GRACE: Maybe you can get a refund? It's an honest mistake. I'm sure people come from all kinds of time zones and get confused.

BARRY: I need a drink. How's the bar here?

TYFFYNI: We have several bars and lounges on property, all well-stocked with a variety of beer, wine, and liquor.

BARRY: Beer. Alright. Hope it ain't all that fancy foreign shit.

TYFFYNI: I'm told we have a good selection of domestics on tap.

BARRY: *(takes special interest in TYFFYNI)* Alright, alright. What'd you got going on later, darlin'? How 'bout you let me buy you a drink after you get off tonight? Or maybe before you get off, wink-wink.

TYFFYNI: Hotel staff aren't permitted to socialize with guests, sir.

BARRY: We'll have to see about changing those rules.

PRISCILLA-GRACE: I think I saw a sign for Jimmy Buffet karaoke tonight, just after the hypnotist. I'm a little bit of a Parrothead myself, but I guess you can't help but be one living in our part of the South. I'm from Mobile, not far from you!

BARRY: *(to TYFFYNI)* So, hey, darlin', you ever been to the Fun Spot?

TYFFYNI: No, sir.

BARRY: You like rides?

TYFFYNI: I get motion sickness.

BARRY: That's cuz you need somebody holding you tight around those bumps and curves.

PRISCILLA-GRACE: We were just talking about how people who live here don't do all these tourist things. She's not on vacation like us.

BARRY: *(to TYFFYNI)* You're too pretty to be working here — what's your name?

BARRY leans in way too close to read TYFFYNI's name tag.

BARRY: Tyffyni with two Ys? Don't see that name much. Exotic. Like a dancer.

TYFFYNI: It's a family name.

PRISCILLA-GRACE: Mamas are so funny about naming their babies, aren't they? My mama named me Priscilla-Grace, on account of she was a huge Elvis Presley fan. I think she loved Elvis more than Daddy loved Walt Disney. Huh. I'm mighty fortunate it was Mama who named me 'cause heaven knows what Daddy would've called me.

BARRY and TYFFYNI stare at PRISCILLA-GRACE for a beat.
BARRY turns his attention back to TYFFYNI.

BARRY: Tyffyni, you're too pretty to be working this desk. You know, you oughta get a job at that murder mystery place. I went yesterday and all them girls they got is ugly and fat. You been there? It's one of those comedy places, there ain't really a murder or anything, just a buncha people doing jokes and dumb shit. Don't get me wrong, them ugly girls were real good at doing jokes. Ugly girls gotta be funny, I reckon.

TYFFYNI: I'm not an actor, sir.

BARRY: You'd be a good actress, I bet. You got a build that'd look real good on a stage. A buddy of mine when to this place a while back, here in Orlando, where the girls did Shakespeare completely naked. You heard of it?

TYFFYNI: That place closed a long time ago.

BARRY: What a shame. I ain't much for the-ate-ter, but I woulda gone for that.

PRISCILLA-GRACE: Lots of other places are still open. Margaritaville's got an all-day happy hour going right now. And Miss Tyffyni here probably needs to focus on helping other guests.

BARRY: I don't see nobody else.

PRISCILLA-GRACE: Just in case somebody comes in—

BARRY: Why don't you take over, lady? You keep butting in with all kinda information nobody asking for.

TYFFYNI: I do have to remain here for our other guests.

BARRY picks up a handful of random brochures and flips through them.

BARRY: Alright, darlin', help me find something to do while we wait for them other guests. Should I go to the Orlando pottery museum — this says they've got a great collection of jugs. Or how about the 4D movie that guarantees a thrilling experience in every seat?

TYFFYNI: *(losing her cool)* There's a Jimmy Buffet sing-along starting at the pool bar in fifteen minutes!

BARRY: You gonna go to that?

TYFFYNI: I am on duty here, sir!

BARRY: We'll tell 'em you're there givin' me information.

TYFFYNI: I cannot leave my station.

BARRY: Shouldn't y'all be concerned about customer satisfaction? I'm a paying customer and I need to be satisfied.

PRISCILLA-GRACE: You are being real inappropriate, mister. Do I need to get the manager?

BARRY: This ain't your business, hun.

TYFFYNI: The manager *would* be happy to assist you, sir.

BARRY: Maybe I'll go to 'im first. *(grabs a comment card from the desk)* I'll fill out this little card about how you mistreated me here. Your boss'll be happy that you've been *unhospitable* with me?

PRISCILLA-GRACE: It's time to leave Miss Tyffyni alone now.

BARRY: *(to TYFFYNI)* This one's just jealous cuz I ain't hitting on her. *(to PRISCILLA-GRACE)* You so desperate for a man's attention that you'll fight with this girl? You've been nagging at me since I got here. No offense, hun, but you ain't my type.

PRISCILLA-GRACE: This poor girl is doing her job and you're bothering her. She's not interested in you, and even if she was, she has still got to be professional here. Why don't you go try and pick up women somewhere else, *hun*?

BARRY: I said butt out, *bitch*.

PRISCILLA-GRACE, flustered, backs off and looks around for help.
BARRY finishes filling out the comment card and leans in close to TYFFYNI.

BARRY: When you're ready to experience a real man, you be in touch. I'll be waiting, sugar tits.

PRISCILLA-GRACE reaches into her bag and pulls out a small plastic baggie. She opens the baggie and tosses the contents into BARRY's face. While BARRY reacts to the dust in his face, TYFFYNI dials the hotel phone and speaks quietly into the receiver.

BARRY: Jesus Christ! You goddamn psycho.

PRISCILLA-GRACE: Your mama should've taught you to be more respectful to women.

TYFFYNI: Hotel security is on their way to escort you from the premises.

BARRY: I'll have you arrested! I'll put you both in jail! You ain't getting away with this! Y'all all gonna pay.

BARRY runs off.
TYFFYNI and PRISCILLA-GRACE watch as BARRY is tackled offstage.

BARRY: *(offstage)* This is bullshit! I ain't done nothing. Get off me! I'll be back, bitches!

TYFFYNI and PRISCILLA-GRACE relax and exhale.

PRISCILLA-GRACE: You okay?

TYFFYNI: We get guys like him sometimes. I'm sorry you scattered your dad like that.

PRISCILLA-GRACE: Oh, there's plenty more of him. If he still had fists, Daddy would have plumb socked the S.O.B. He never tolerated that sort.

TYFFYNI: Thank you.

PRISCILLA-GRACE: We got to look out for each other, don't we?

TYFFYNI: Mhmm.

PRISCILLA-GRACE: Do I need a reservation for that murder mystery thing?

TYFFYNI: Let me handle that for you.

END OF SCENE. BLACKOUT.

CURSE OF THE KIGURUMI

Three friends return to their hotel room from a convention after someone in their group has been turned into a sock monkey by what they believe to be a real witch.

(Kigurumi [kee-goo-ROO-mee] is a Japanese portmanteau that means "to wear a stuffed toy." The costume is generally hooded onesie pajamas designed to look like cute animals like unicorns, pandas, cats, etc.)

(The three main characters have no gender or race ascribed to them in order to encourage flexibility in casting. Character action uses they/their pronouns. The unseen/non-speaking characters have been gendered, but their relationships to the characters should not influence gender in casting.)

<u>CAST</u>:
ALEX - sensible, dressed in a puppy kigurumi
JAMIE - sensitive, dressed in a bunny kigurumi
DYLAN - sardonic, dressed in a panda kigurumi
CHARLIE - a sock monkey

SETTING: *A hotel room in the Belle Royale Palm Vista Plaza Conference Resort and Suites of Orlando*

Three people in animal onesies and in various states of distress, enter their hotel room. JAMIE is carrying a sock monkey (CHARLIE).

DYLAN: *(groans)* Oh, boy.

JAMIE: This is bad.

ALEX: Let's not panic.

JAMIE: What're we gonna do?

DYLAN: What can we do?

ALEX: We'll work it out somehow. Take a breath, have a seat.

JAMIE: How can you be so calm? It's not every day a witch curses a guy and turns him into a sock monkey.

DYLAN: Well, just because we don't hear about it doesn't mean it's not happening. I mean, witches are probably out there transforming people into inanimate objects and whatnot all the time. It is kind of their job.

ALEX: When was the last time you saw jobs for witches in the want ads?

DYLAN: They're probably independent contractors, like plumbers or wedding photographers or hit-men.

JAMIE: I've seen ads looking for wizards.

ALEX: Wizards or witches?

JAMIE: What's the difference?

ALEX: Witches are female, wizards are male.

DYLAN: I thought warlocks were male witches.

ALEX: What are wizards?

DYLAN: Wizards are from ancient, like, medieval times, with the long beards and robes.

ALEX: But who cursed Charlie?

JAMIE: It all happened so fast.

DYLAN: Definitely a witch.

ALEX: You're sure?

DYLAN: Yeah, she was this crotchety old hag or an old gypsy crone.

ALEX: The word "gypsy" is a slur.

DYLAN: Since when?

ALEX: Probably since ever, but definitely now.

DYLAN: What about "hag"? Or "crone"?

ALEX: I don't know. They aren't exactly flattering.

DYLAN: What about "witch"?

ALEX: I confess, I'm ignorant of the PC terminology for people who practice magic, professionally or otherwise.

DYLAN: This is precisely the sort of cultural insensitivity that got Charlie into his situation.

JAMIE: What're we gonna do? Should we find the witch?

ALEX: We should at least report the incident to someone. *(pulls out phone)* I'll contact the convention organizers.

ALEX steps away to talk on their phone.

DYLAN: Who's gonna believe that a guy dressed as a sock monkey intentionally shoulder-bumped a witch at an anime convention while calling her an offensive slur, causing her to cast a spell that turned him into a toy sock monkey? Just saying it out loud now sounds ludicrous.

JAMIE: If this witch is going around cursing other people, isn't it our duty to report this so she can be stopped?

DYLAN: *(pulls out phone)* I'm texting Casey. I don't want her to freak out when she gets back from the outlet mall.

DYLAN snaps photo of JAMIE cradling CHARLIE.

JAMIE: Oh, Charlie, what are we gonna do with you?

DYLAN: *(to JAMIE, while texting)* He got what he deserved.

JAMIE: You think he deserved to be cursed like this?

DYLAN: He's always a jerk — catcalling women, leaving the toilet seat up, taunting the physically challenged, eating the last slice of pizza without asking, singing "Sweet Home Alabama" three times in a row at karaoke. I don't know why we keep hanging out with the guy.

ALEX: *(still on their phone)* He buys the pizza.

JAMIE: And he's our friend.

DYLAN: For all we know, the curse'll wear off any minute. And you'll be cursed with a broken back.

ALEX: Okay, the convention organizer says they haven't heard about any other incidents like ours but will keep a look out. They say the witch we encountered might have been someone going to Hex-a-Con, the magical practitioners conference in the hotel next door.

JAMIE: Let's go!

DYLAN: This is really not how I wanted to spend my weekend.

JAMIE: Why are you so resistant to helping one of your oldest friends? Is it because of Casey?

DYLAN: Hey, he's the one who got himself mixed up with some petty witch. And for the record, Casey didn't leave him for me. She left him, then, after a respectable amount of time, she and I organically upgraded our friendship. If anyone's still holding a grudge, it's Charlie.

ALEX: Should we be talking about him like he's not in the room?

DYLAN: Can he even hear us? He's a toy now. Aren't his insides made of polyfill fibers?

JAMIE: What if it's not him? The witch made a lot of smoke when Charlie disappeared. They could've kidnapped him and left this behind.

DYLAN: Or killed him. That could be his corpse.

JAMIE drops the sock monkey on the floor, then quickly scoops him up and wordlessly apologizes, hugging him closer.

ALEX: Don't be so macabre, Dylan! There's a difference between being turned into a toy and being murdered. We don't know how magic works. Maybe the curse transformed him by radically altering his DNA or he could be shrunk down and trapped inside the toy.

DYLAN: How is magic so far advanced than science and yet we don't have flying cars and stuff?

ALEX: Because magic is perceived as a feminine practice and casual misogyny has maligned it as a profession and a lifestyle, which is why we don't see major corporations hiring in-house sorcerers. Eradicate the patriarchy and then we can have flying cars.

DYLAN: Boy, Charlie would've had a field day with that theory.

JAMIE: He's right here!

DYLAN: If only he'd been dressed as Tarzan, we'd know for sure. Whose idea was it for us to wear animal onesies?

JAMIE: Charlie bought these for us. He thought it'd be funny to meet washed-up action stars while dressed in fuzzy pajamas.

DYLAN: Oh, right. Why was Steven Seagal even signing autographs at an anime convention?

ALEX: Logic doesn't really apply at these events. *(scratching behind their puppy costume ear)* These onesies are so itchy. I might've cursed Charlie myself.

DYLAN: Let's say the curse is like being in a coma. Whether he's trapped or transformed, he can hear still us but he can't respond normally?

DYLAN takes the sock monkey from JAMIE and places it on the table.

DYLAN: Hello, Charlie? Can you hear me? If you're in there, try tapping the table — twice for yes and once for no.

Two knocks on table.

JAMIE: Whoa.

DYLAN: Alright, somebody call the witch doctor!

ALEX: That's definitely offensive. I'll check my phone for an antidote, like a potion or something. Like you said, witches could be cursing people all the time.

DYLAN: Yeah, I'm sure room service will bring us a cauldron and eye of newt.

While JAMIE and DYLAN engage in discussion, ALEX continues to look at their phone and sporadically displays puppy-like tics, like yipping or panting.

JAMIE: Sometimes curses can be broken by true love's kiss.

DYLAN: Be my guest, James.

JAMIE: Do you think he learned his lesson?

DYLAN: *(to sock monkey)* Charlie, have you learned to stop being a rude bastard?

Two quick knocks on table.

JAMIE: He said yes.

DYLAN: Doesn't seem sincere. He hasn't had time to be humbled by the experience.

JAMIE: You don't know how he feels. He can't be comfortable being trapped.

DYLAN: Let's find out. Give him a big ol' smooch!

JAMIE notices ALEX trying to use their leg to scratch behind their ear.

JAMIE: Are you okay, Alex?

ALEX: I'm fine. *(yips)* I haven't found anything to help Charlie yet. *(snaps up, looks alert)* Is that a squirrel?

DYLAN: Oh, boy.

JAMIE: Did the witch curse you, too?

ALEX: Of course not. *(woof)* That's ridiculous! *(arf)* I would've changed when he did, right?

DYLAN: Maybe the costumes are cursed.

ALEX: We should take these *(woof)*-ing things off already.

ALEX and JAMIE try their costume zippers.

ALEX: The zippers are stuck. *(arf)*

JAMIE: Do we have any scissors?

JAMIE starts frantically looking around the room.

DYLAN: Where did Charlie get these things?

ALEX: He ordered them from Amazon.

DYLAN: Must've been a third-party seller.

ALEX snarls and bites at their zipper.

DYLAN: You're not looking like yourself, Al. Go take a look in the mirror.

ALEX exits and is heard barking repeatedly and growling off-stage. A clap of thunder accompanies the flickering of lights. The barking stops. DYLAN and JAMIE freeze.
JAMIE exits for a beat, then returns with a stuffed puppy that looks like ALEX's costume.

JAMIE: Why is this happening?!

DYLAN: That's it. I'm gonna go over to Hex-a-Con and look for a witch or a wizard or a shaman to fix all of this. Casey is on her way now. You can wait here for her.

JAMIE: What is she gonna think about all this?

DYLAN uses their own phone to take photo of JAMIE with puppy ALEX.

DYLAN: She thought it was all a joke at first. But when I sent her the pic of you mooning over that sock monkey like you do with the real Charlie, she was convinced. Love like that doesn't lie.

JAMIE: Shhhh!

DYLAN: You're in love with Charlie. Everybody knows it. Well, now everybody knows.

JAMIE: I didn't want it to come out this way.

DYLAN: No one could've ever imagined that this was a way for it to come out. Who knows, once we break the curse, there might be a happily ever after for you two.

JAMIE sets puppy ALEX on the table next to sock monkey CHARLIE. DYLAN grabs ALEX's phone and searches through it.

DYLAN: If I run, I can catch the end of the seminar on Brand Awareness for Freelance Magical Practitioners. You're gonna be okay here?

JAMIE: I'm starting to feel a little bunny-like.

DYLAN: Just…try to think non-bunny thoughts.

JAMIE: *(twitches nose like a bunny)* Aren't you worried about transforming, too?

DYLAN: Charlie, the bastard, didn't buy a kigurumi for me. He was probably still feeling burned about the whole Casey break-up— *(to sock monkey)* Even though she left you because you're a selfish, cheating jerk!— *(to JAMIE)* Sorry, I know. Anyway. You guys all got pizza and pajamas and I got this off the clearance rack at Target.

DYLAN tugs at the zipper on their costume and it unzips easily. JAMIE twitches their nose. DYLAN takes a few more photos of their friends with their phone.

DYLAN: Okay, let's see if I can convince someone to skip Witches' Brew happy hour to undo this voodoo.

DYLAN exits the room. JAMIE looks at the stuffed puppy and sock monkey on the table. JAMIE turns the puppy facing away and then picks up the sock monkey. They pucker up and kiss the sock monkey's face.
A clap of thunder accompanies a quick flicker of light and blackout.

END OF SCENE.

Katharine Miller

TOURIST TRAPPED

A female pianist entertains convention guests.

CAST:
AGNES - (20s/30s) wearing black pants and a vaguely tiki-themed, tropical print blouse, sits behind piano or keyboard

ROCK STAR with conference badge on lanyard for BizDev Summit
NINJA with conference badge on lanyard for BizDev Summit
GURU with conference badge on lanyard for BizDev Summit

SETTING: A tiki-themed cocktail lounge at the Belle Royale Palm Vista Plaza Conference Resort and Suites of Orlando

As AGNES plays the final chords of "Margaritaville", the audience lightly applauds. She noodles around on the piano, alternating between the opening bars and the chorus of "The Girl From Ipanema", as she leisurely talks to the crowd.

AGNES: Thank you. And again, thanks for joining me here in the Tacky Tiki at the beautiful Belle Royale Palm Vista Plaza Conference Resort and Suites of Orlando. If this is your first visit to Orlando, welcome. You may not know that, a long time ago, all of this used to be orange groves. My mother loved to tell me that when we would come here on family vacations. She'd talk about how people driving along would stop their cars on the side of the road and pick oranges right off the trees. "That was before ol' Walt came in and built our paradise," she'd say. The orange groves, if they did exist, are long gone, paved over with highways that are decorated with billboards for two-bit novelty attractions and the occasional religious message. Three-dimensional signs lunge out from the roadside to promote the newest attractions and assure travellers that they haven't wasted their valuable tourist dollars by choosing to spend the hottest days of the year battling heat stroke and humidity, endless queues, and the occasional hurricane. This weekend at the Tacky Tiki, all specialty cocktails come in a Tacky Tiki souvenir hurricane glass, just $16.99, while supplies last.

AGNES plays a recognizable snippet from "Aloha Oe" and returns to "The Girl From Ipanema".

AGNES: That last song was a request from the the fine folks visiting from the BizDev Summit.

The costumed characters cheer and whoop, then resumed their muted conversation amongst themselves.

AGNES: I don't know if you recognized it, one of the deep cuts from Jimmy Buffet's 1977 album *Changes in Latitudes, Changes in Attitudes.* Since the discovery of the Fountain of Youth, people have flocked here to America's wang for respite from the humdrum and doldrums of everyday life. Florida is 65,755 square miles of escapism. For people who like piña coladas and getting caught in the rain, there's no better destination. Leave reality behind for a week and pretend that your life is all margaritas and mojitos, sunshine and shuffleboard.

AGNES plays a recognizable snippet of "Escape (The Piña Colada Song)" that can segue into a recognizable snippet "It's a Small World" and returns to "The Girl From Ipanema".

AGNES: Not content to knock one back with Parrotheads and retirees, Ol' Walt and his successors tamed the wild wetland — and transformed it into a Fantasyland, a Sea World, a whole stinking universe, where all your dreams can come true — provided those dreams were part of an animated feature-length film. Thanks to pixie dust and a generous credit card limit, the ordinary can be extraordinary. The wicked stepsisters become Cinderella, the sidekicks become superheroes, the lost boys find new hope as stormtroopers. In Orlando, universes collide and alternate timelines merge so that you can be anywhere but here and now. Don't miss the Fanmageddon Doctor Who Q&A panel in the Diamond Pineapple room at 7:15 tonight.

AGNES plays a recognizable snippet of the Doctor Who *theme and returns to "The Girl From Ipanema".*

AGNES: Theme parks offer the closest thing we mortals have to time travel. Mass transit vehicles alternately creak and zoom through meticulously designed environments. Everyone stands fanny pack to fanny pack with fellow escapees who've spent a month's rent for a weekend of theoretical pleasure. The Vacation Dads moan about the cost of everything and insist on squeezing as much "fun" out of the experience to get their money's worth. When they aren't complaining about money, they explain obscure references in excruciating detail. They make up theme park trivia to pass the time in queues. They make a show of trying to be funnier than 19-year-old Jungle Cruise skippers reciting the 50-year-old Jungle Cruise jokes.

AGNES plays a recognizable snippet of the Gilligan's Island *theme and returns to "The Girl From Ipanema".*

AGNES: The Vacation Moms insist on manufacturing magic moments for their children, often at the risk of mangling magic moments for everyone else. They are always 90 seconds away from a meltdown. There is no escape for the Vacation Moms, whose duties are reminding their children of the songs from that one movie and standing in the sweltering heat to pose the children with the characters from that other movie. The Vacation Moms bark orders at their children like drill sergeant cheerleaders — "Look, Madison, it's your princess! Smile, McKinley! Wave to Mickey Mouse, Taylor. Get Dory to sign your autograph book, Buchanan. Give Pinocchio a kiss, Nixon!" Ol' Walt never imagined his parks filled with little white girls named after American presidents, but he probably wouldn't complain about it.

AGNES plays a recognizable snippet of "Be Our Guest" and returns to "The Girl From Ipanema".

AGNES: Whatever brings you to Orlando, I hope you're having a good time. Lots of people come to Orlando for a weekend and have such a good time that they decide to stay on permanent vacation. Something in the reclaimed water, maybe. It's impossible to do everything in one weekend. You could live here a year and still never be able to experience it all — what with sitting in traffic and hustling between jobs to afford the cost of living. Only the independently wealthy can enjoy the life of a perpetual tourist. The rest of us get jobs in the places we love and learn to hate every square inch.

AGNES plays a recognizable snippet of "Working For the Weekend" and returns to "The Girl From Ipanema".

AGNES: Living next door to Fantasyland is no dream come true. No amount of pixie dust seems to ease the traffic on I-4. The only Magic is in the arena on Saturday nights — if your idea of enchantment is a bunch of guys dribbling in shorts. The cracks in the facade of the artifice of this paradise are deepening. There are lizards on the sidewalk, frogs in the jacuzzi, and 'gators on the golf course. Eventually, the bloom falls off the animatronic rose. Before you say "Sayonara, Sunshine State", check out the vintage postcard display in the hotel gift shop to see Orlando in all its orange-groved glory.

AGNES plays the opening to "The Rainbow Connection".

AGNES: Everybody you meet in this town is wearing some kind of costume, chasing some kind of dream. This next song is dedicated to all the colourful characters here at the Belle Royale Palm Vista Plaza Conference Resort and Suites of Orlando.

END OF SCENE. BLACK OUT.

NO CONTEXT

The awkwardness of getting recognized in a public place.

CAST:
BEN - stock photo guy dressed in cliche tourist garb, loud Hawaiian print shirt, khaki shorts and sandals, Panama hat and sunglasses
MARK - cosplay geek, dressed as Sherlock Holmes with multiple convention lanyards
BRIAN - janitor, in jumpsuit with lanyard for Belle Royale Palm Vista Plaza Conference Resort and Suites

SETTING: *A public men's restroom in the Belle Royale Palm Vista Plaza Conference Resort and Suites of Orlando*

BEN *and* MARK *are washing their hands in the public restroom.* MARK *repeatedly looks over at* BEN, *who gets a little unnerved and checks his reflection in the mirror.*

MARK: Great look.

BEN: Thanks?

MARK: What's it from?

BEN: Where — um, Tommy Bahama, I think.

MARK: Tommy Bahama — is he like Magnum P.I.?

BEN: I don't know what you're talking about.

MARK: Most people at this convention go overboard on costumes. Yours is nice. Subtle. Maybe too subtle. I can't quite tell who you're supposed to be.

BEN: This isn't a costume, Sherlock. My wife bought this for me at the mall, for our vacation.

MARK: You're not in costume?

BEN: Nope. Just "tourist on vacation."

BEN grabs a paper towel to dry his hands. MARK continues to stare at BEN.

MARK: You look familiar, though.

BEN: I get that a lot. Just one of those faces.

MARK: Where do I know you from?

BEN: You've seen me around the hotel.

MARK: Hmm. I feel like I've seen you before this weekend.

BEN: Maybe we were on the same airport shuttle.

MARK: This is gonna bug me.

BEN shrugs and moves to exit the restroom.

MARK: Wait — you're that guy!

MARK intercepts BEN before he can open the door.

BEN: No.

MARK: You are!

BEN: No.

MARK: C'mon!

BEN: Whoever you think I am — I'm not.

BEN reaches for the door.

MARK: Yeah, from the meme.

BEN freezes.

BEN: Oh, god.

MARK: The picture of the scared guy running away from the clown — you're that guy!

BEN: I wasn't running away. The clown was chasing me.

MARK gets out his camera/phone and grabs BEN's shoulder to pull him in closer for a photo.

MARK: Can I get a selfie with you?

BEN ducks and moves away.

BEN: I'd rather not.

MARK: C'mon! We'll do the meme. I'll be the clown.
(strikes a menacing pose)

BEN: Please—

MARK: Okay, I'll be you and you be the clown.
(strikes "mock terrified in mid-run" pose)

BEN: No, it's —

MARK: It'd be better if I'm in my underpants, like you were. *(starts to pull down pants)*

BEN: Jesus — STOP!

MARK: Alright, alright. Most people are flattered to be recognized.

BEN: I'm not most people.

MARK: No, you're famous!

BEN: I'm really not.

MARK: Don't sell yourself short. Internet fame is just as valid as the other kind.

BEN: I don't want to be Internet famous. I can't help that the photo went viral.

MARK: You're beyond mere viral sensation. You're evergreen content, son!

BEN: Ugh.

MARK: I've heard the Ellen show is looking for you and the clown.

BEN: What does Ellen Degeneres want with me and Ralph?

MARK: To make you TV famous, my friend.

BEN: We don't want to be TV famous. It's bad for our business.

MARK: What kind of business could possibly be damaged by more publicity? *(stage whispers)* Is it drugs?

BEN: We're professional stock photo models.

MARK: Oh? Well, stock photo memes are all the rage now. You're gonna be bigger than Distracted Boyfriend and Ladies Laughing at Salads.

BEN: Our careers will be over. We'll never be hired again.

MARK: How do you figure?

BEN: Stock photography relies on a certain level of anonymity. To be a successful stock model, we need to have an average, inoffensive familiarity about us. Engaging enough to get people interested in whatever some corporation has decided we should represent, but forgettable enough that no one gets curious about our actual lives. You know the photo of the guy that comes with all the picture frames?

MARK: Yeah.

BEN: That's me.

MARK: Oh! *Of course!*

BEN: Or, rather, it used to be me. Last week, my wife bought a new picture frame and, for the first time in 20 years, had to put my photo *in* it.

MARK pulls out his wallet and finds that he has BEN's picture in his wallet's photo insert. BEN is unsure how to react to this discovery.

MARK: *(comparing BEN to his photo)* You think that's blowback from the meme and not the fact that feathered bangs and frosted tips went out of style ages ago? Would you autograph this for me?

MARK fishes a pen out of his bag and BEN reluctantly takes the pen and scribbles on the picture.

MARK: Huh. You don't look like a Ben. *(puts his stuff back in his bag)* So, if you're so big into being average and inoffensive, why pose naked with a clown?

BEN: *(groans)* I wasn't entirely naked. Our photographer wanted some edgier pieces to add to his portfolio. He *is* trying to break out of the stocks, ironically, but no one's staring at him in public restrooms.

MARK: Touché. You're racking up mad bank from the meme, though, right?

BEN: Nope. Doesn't matter if an insurance company uses the image once or the whole of the Internet shares it indefinitely, my job is done and my fee is paid.

MARK: You need a better agent. Don't you think you're entitled to some financial benefit?

BEN: I've done all right coasting on my generic good looks. Enough to bring my family on a summer vacation to Walt Disney World every year, which I really should get back to now, if you don't mind.

MARK: *(pulls business card out of backpack)* I know I don't look it, but I'm a lawyer. If you want, I could negotiate for you, get you a cut of the profits. No reason why those clickbait sites should get all the dough.

BEN: I'll think about it, thanks. Do me a favour? Please, don't tell anyone you saw me.

MARK: Your identity is safe with me.

BEN exits the restroom.
BRIAN enters.

BRIAN: Awesome costume, man.

MARK: Thanks!

BRIAN: Here for Fanmageddon?

MARK: *(flashes convention lanyard)* Yep. You? Lemme guess — you're a ghostbuster, right?

BRIAN: *(flashes hotel ID lanyard)* Nah. Hotel janitor.

MARK: Damn. 0 for two.

BRIAN: Hey, the guy who just left, was he—?

MARK: Yep. He's the guy in the photo that comes with all the picture frames.

BRIAN: Oh, yeah! Doesn't he kinda look like that naked guy from the meme, though? With the clown?

MARK: He's just got that kind of face, I guess.

BRIAN: Guess so. Welp, these johns aren't gonna scrub themselves.

MARK: Right. Vaya con dios.

BRIAN: Piso mojado.

MARK exits.
BRIAN checks under the stalls, then turns to face the mirror. He pulls his jumpsuit open to reveal a superhero costume.

BRIAN: Well, if it isn't my evil nemesis. *(turns dramatically to face the toilets)* Stall number three — we meet again.

END OF SCENE. BLACK OUT.

SOUVENIRS

A vacationing couple are grilled by the hotel detective over suspicious activity.

CAST:
BEVERLY - (50s+) hotel guest, wife, casual wear under a plush hotel robe, clutching a tote bag with a price tag obviously still attached.
KEITH - (50s+) hotel guest, husband, casual wear under a plush hotel robe, wearing a floppy sun hat with a price tag obviously still attached.
HANNAH - (30-40s) hotel detective, business casual or plainclothes cop attire

SETTING: *The investigations office in the Belle Royale Palm Vista Plaza Conference Resort and Suites of Orlando*

BEVERLY and KEITH, *both wrapped in plush hotel bathrobes, sit in chairs, sulking. HANNAH is perched on top of her desk across from the couple.*

HANNAH: Whenever you're ready.

BEVERLY: We told you.

HANNAH: Tell me again.

KEITH: You can't treat us this way. We're guests here.

HANNAH: It's a routine inquiry. Just answer my questions and we can all move on. So, please, again, tell me where were you taking your luggage in such a rush at eight o'clock tonight?

BEVERLY: To our car.   KEITH: For a walk.

HANNAH: For a walk? To your car?

BEVERLY and KEITH: Yes.

HANNAH: In bathrobes?

BEVERLY: I was cold.   KEITH: We were going to the pool.

HANNAH: Where are your swimsuits?

BEVERLY: Under our clothes.   KEITH: In our luggage.

HANNAH: Uh huh.

KEITH: I don't know why you refuse to believe us.

HANNAH: You don't? Let's see. First, you told me you were on your way to a "costume convention" dressed as "hotel guests".

KEITH: We have passes for Vacation-Con but I left them in my other pants.

HANNAH: And then you said you were on your way to the hotel spa for a couples massage and felt unsafe leaving your luggage in your room.

KEITH: Look, we just wanna leave Orlando and get home before the storm hits.

BEVERLY: Yes! We were loading up the car so we could get on the road, try to beat the hurricane traffic…

HANNAH: And now it's a hurricane! Well, the storm's over. It fizzled out near the Bahamas.

BEVERLY: Oh, what a relief!

HANNAH: Let's see if I've got this now — you're eager to get out of town, but you were going to stop for a massage, maybe a swim, and attend a convention first?

KEITH: Who are you to judge how people spend their vacations, the... vacation... police?

HANNAH: I'm the hotel's in-house detective.

BEVERLY: I didn't know hotels still had detectives. How quaint!

HANNAH: Those robes—

KEITH: We brought them from home.

HANNAH: You expect me to believe those bathrobes with the "Belle Royale Palm Vista Plaza Conference Resort and Suites" embroidered logo are yours that you brought from home to stay at this very hotel?

BEVERLY: We're big fans.

KEITH: We bought 'em off the hotel website.

HANNAH: Uh huh.

HANNAH moves to one of the large pieces of luggage. She pushes it flat onto the floor, unzips it and squats down to pick through the contents.

HANNAH: Is that also where you got this clock radio, this Gideon Bible, these wooden anti-theft hangers, this "Belle Royale Palm Vista Plaza Conference Resort and Suites" branded ice bucket, and these lavender-infused memory foam pillows?

BEVERLY: There was a sale.

HANNAH pulls an origami folded towel out of the luggage.

HANNAH: And this towel swan?

KEITH: *(grabs for the towel)* That's my emotional support towel swan!

HANNAH: What's his name?

KEITH: *(hugging the towel swan tightly)* Her name is suh…wan…nee.

HANNAH: Swanee?

KEITH: Y'know, like from the song. *(sings)* "Way down upon the S'wannee River —" *(normal)* Hey, isn't that river around here somewhere?

HANNAH: You wanna know what I think?

BEVERLY: No ma'am.

HANNAH: I think you're a couple of liars here. Yep. You're liars and thieves looking to rip off this hotel.

KEITH: Even if that were true, the hotel can afford it. You ever heard of insurance?

HANNAH: You ever heard of jail?

BEVERLY: *(flustered)* I'd like to speak to your manager!

HANNAH: You'd like to speak to the manager.

BEVERLY: Yes. I'm sure we can straighten all of this out with him.

HANNAH: Oh, sure, we'll bring in the manager and you can explain to him that this is all one big misunderstanding. You can tell him about costumes and massages and how everything in your luggage looks identical to the things kept in our rooms but is actually stuff you got off the hotel's online store and brought with you from home — why, exactly?

KEITH: We're germaphobes.

HANNAH: Of course you are!

KEITH: The 45th president of the United States is a noted germaphobe who travels with his monogrammed bathrobe and he only stays at hotels that he owns.

BEVERLY: What if we return all the stuff in this bag? Can we forget the whole thing?

HANNAH: You wanna return all this stuff? What — to the online store for a refund, I suppose? And, uh, what about the other bag?

KEITH: Nothing there but a couple of keepsakes.

HANNAH unzips the luggage to find all sorts of tacky Florida souvenirs. KEITH and BEVERLY cringe and hide their faces in embarrassment.

HANNAH: Airbrushed t-shirts, picture postcards, novelty snow globes, inflatable palm trees, flamingo bobbleheads, alligator keychains...

KEITH: Aren't we allowed to have souvenirs?

HANNAH: It looks like you cleaned out the whole gift shop.

BEVERLY: We've got a lot of family back home.

HANNAH: You gonna tell me you bought this stuff on sale, too? The hotel has security video that says otherwise.

HANNAH turns the computer screen on her desk to face the couple and presses a key to start the video of the couple shoplifting.

BEVERLY: Is that us?

HANNAH: Yep.

BEVERLY: It looks like we're smuggling things out of the store!

HANNAH: Because you are. And doing a terrible job of hiding it.

KEITH: *(indignant)* I have no memory of doing this. This is obviously doctored footage. Beverly is not that fat and I would never wear such a ridiculous hat!

BEVERLY reaches over and pulls the sun hat off of KEITH's head.

KEITH: *(stammering)* You know what this is — profiling — ageism. Yes! You think our generation just goes around taking things and —

BEVERLY: *(sighs)* Keith! Let's just tell her the truth.

KEITH: She'll never believe us, Bev.

BEVERLY: *(to Hannah)* We were hypnotized—

KEITH: By the hotel's hypnotist—

BEVERLY: We went to his show last night and he pulled us out of the audience, then put us in a trance to make us steal all these things.

HANNAH: Oh, brother.

KEITH: And he said, "When you hear the phrase 'Excuse me, where do you think you're going with that?' you'll snap out of it."

HANNAH: He make you sing like Elvis, too?

KEITH: I knew you wouldn't believe it.

HANNAH: I believe you.

BEVERLY and KEITH: *(stunned and flabbergasted)* What?! Really?!

HANNAH: Yeah, Eddie's always pulling stuff like this. There's a guy up in a room right now thinks he's a cat, the janitor believes he's a superhero, and half of our security guys are out there strutting around like chickens. I swear I spend most of my days sorting out his hypnotic messes. Let me talk to the manager.

HANNAH picks up the phone.

HANNAH: *(on phone)* Yeah, Van? Hannah. Listen, I got a couple shoplifters here claiming to be the work of Eddie. Yep. They looted their room, too. Uh huh. They seem pretty embarrassed about it. You shoulda heard some of their crazy cover stories — Cut 'em loose? No, we don't need more lawsuits. Alright.

HANNAH hangs up and turns back to the couple.

HANNAH: You're free to go.

KEITH: Finally!

BEVERLY: Thank heavens!

HANNAH: For all your troubles, you're welcome to take the robes.

KEITH: And Swanee?

HANNAH: *(rolling her eyes)* Yes, you can keep your towel swan.

KEITH: *(hugging swan tightly)* Thank you.

BEVERLY checks her watch.

BEVERLY: Ooh, if we hurry we can catch the magician's act.

KEITH: Is he any good?

HANNAH: He's great at making people disappear.

BEVERLY: How exciting! Let's go, dear.

BEVERLY and KEITH exit.
HANNAH sits at her desk. The phone rings.

HANNAH: *(on phone)* Investigations — A murder in the karaoke lounge? Someone's slaughtering Billy Joel's "Piano Man"? *(groans)* Ha, ha, Carl. Get back to work.

END OF SCENE. BLACKOUT.

DESCONHECIDO

Two strangers meet after a long day.

CAST:
LINDA - (early 40s/late 30s) acerbic, sarcastic, determined to be kind and upbeat, in casual maxi dress/resortwear
DEREK - a rough-looking guy of indeterminate age with greasy hair, leather jacket and loud print shirt

SETTING: *The cocktail lounge in the Belle Royale Palm Vista Plaza Conference Resort and Suites of Orlando*

DEREK and LINDA are seated at the bar, with one stool between them. They each have ridiculous umbrella drinks. They have clearly been drinking, separately, and their inebriation becomes apparent throughout their conversation.

DEREK studies LINDA as she idly swirls her crazy straw in her cocktail. A piano version of "The Girl from Ipanema" plays in the background.

DEREK: You look normal.

LINDA: Um, thank you?

DEREK: Are you supposed to be someone?

LINDA: *(focused on her cocktail)* The forgiving daughter, obedient sister, all-around saintly woman and plucky heroine in a Hallmark rom-com. *(realizes what he's asking)* There's no costume for that, though.
(turns to DEREK) How about you? Off to pull a heist or is there a Quentin Tarantino fan expo in town?

DEREK: Is it that obvi— ah. No. No, this isn't a costume either.

LINDA: So, a leather jacket in Orlando in July is a personal style choice?

DEREK: Erm. well — it's complicated. So, you're here for a holiday? Business? Pleasure?

LINDA: I'm here with family.

DEREK: Ah. Will your, er, husband being joining you?

LINDA: No husband. Just a Southern Gothic imitation of *Grey Gardens* with less whimsy and far more racial epithets.

DEREK: Ah.

LINDA: It's complicated.

DEREK: Hmm.

LINDA: This wasn't the best first impression. That'll teach you to chat up strange women in hotel bars, I guess.

DEREK: Yeah. But, you know what? I've been mucking things up all day. Care to start over?

LINDA: Yes, actually, I would. Pick up where you tell me how normal I look.

LINDA smiles awkwardly and tries to bat her eyelashes flirtatiously. DEREK hesitates, doubtful of LINDA's sincerity. LINDA nods and motions for him to go-ahead. DEREK moves over to the stool next to LINDA.

DEREK: Um, hi.

LINDA: Hello!

DEREK: What brings you here?

LINDA: I am attending an, uh, intergenerational women's retreat this weekend. It's been a long day of revelation and enlightenment and, now, I'm letting spirits guide me to a state of inebriated bliss.

DEREK: Would you join me in a little celebration?

LINDA: Sure. What are we celebrating?

DEREK: I quit my job today. Well, the whole business really.

LINDA: What'd you do?

DEREK: I was a, er, field directives liaison for an underground redistribution syndicate.

LINDA: Interesting… and what made you quit today?

DEREK: Oh, I botched a job, embarrassed myself in front of a client, and may be personally responsible for unleashing the most dangerous software application onto the free world.

LINDA: *(sarcastic)* Well, that is cause for celebration!

DEREK: Yeah, it sounds bonkers.

LINDA: No. I mean, it takes courage to abandon a job, a career. Good for you.

DEREK: It was always a contract position, no real opportunity for advancement. Now, I can move onto the next phase in my life. I could buy a horse farm or open a record store.

LINDA: My father had a horse farm.

DEREK: Oh?

LINDA: He supplied a lot of raw materials for the local glue factory.

DEREK: Ah.

LINDA: Maybe you'll be more successful. Do you know anything about horses?

DEREK: Only what I've seen on racing forms.

LINDA: Hmm. What do you know about music?

DEREK: I know this lounge pianist has been playing "The Girl from Ipanema" for 15 minutes.

LINDA: Do you think someone paid her to do it?

DEREK: I was in a bar once where someone paid to program the jukebox to play Toto's "Africa" 27 times in a row.

LINDA: Were they trying to break a record?

DEREK: The whole jukebox was smashed to bits.

LINDA: Maybe this song's been an earworm all day and she thinks by playing it, she'll get closure, but she's gotten herself stuck in a loop.

DEREK: Bossa nova is infectious. It'll get you every time.

LINDA: And I thought the rhythm was gonna get me. Ooh! Maybe she's in a hypnotic trance.

DEREK: Or she's an animatronic in need of repair.

LINDA: Or this is the only song she knows how to play.

DEREK: She's probably just biding time until someone makes a request.

LINDA: I'd like to request for her to stop.

DEREK: Alright, I'll go ask for something else. What'd you like to hear?

LINDA: "Africa" by Toto.

DEREK: Funny.

DEREK gets up and starts to cross the bar. The music stops abruptly. DEREK pauses while he and LINDA watch (off-stage) as the pianist leaves.

DEREK and LINDA: *(disappointed)* Aw.

DEREK returns to his seat next to LINDA.

LINDA: Was it something we said?

DEREK: We broke the spell she was under.

LINDA: Well done, us!

DEREK and LINDA high five. LINDA sees ink on DEREK's palm. She grabs his hand and reads what's written on it.

LINDA: What is "the toxic funk will crash tonight"?

DEREK: The mark of the end of my career.

LINDA: The Toxic Funk sounds like a comic book super-villain.

DEREK: He kind of is, actually.

LINDA: So, does that make you a superhero?

DEREK: More like a super coward.

LINDA: Ah. Well, at least you don't have to wear so much spandex. Here's to that. *(raises glass, noisily slurps her drink through the crazy straw.)* Hey, where is Ipanema?

DEREK: Wha— I dunno. Africa? Costa Rica? No, wait, Brazil.

LINDA: I think I'd like to go to Brazil some day.

DEREK: Let's go.

LINDA: Right now?

DEREK: Why not?

LINDA: So many reasons. One, I don't have my passport.

DEREK: I can get you a passport.

LINDA: I don't speak the language or have the proper currency. I'm not wearing appropriate shoes.

DEREK: Those aren't reasons to not go, those are details to handle on the way. Do you need special shoes for Brazil?

LINDA: I meant for travel in general. I don't know if Brazil has a dress code. I mean, they are famous for bikini waxes, but maybe they wax for practicality, not for show.

DEREK: From what I've seen of Rio, they seem to be fairly casual.

LINDA: You've been to Rio?

DEREK: Only in my fantasies.

LINDA: Maybe we should stick to our fantasies a while longer.

DEREK: Your mum won't let you run off with a man you've just met, eh?

LINDA: My mother thinks I shouldn't eat popcorn and hard candy because she thinks they're choking hazards.

DEREK: I've got popcorn on my boat.

LINDA: You've got a boat? I'm sold, let's go.

DEREK: Do you have boat shoes?

LINDA: Not on me. Drat.

DEREK: Alright, we'll stop for boat shoes on the way to Tampa.

LINDA: I thought we were going to Brazil.

DEREK: My boat's in Tampa.

LINDA: I have so many questions.

DEREK: I'll tell you almost anything you want to know, but I'm afraid you'll change your mind.

LINDA: Okay, why don't you tell me about your boat over a shrimp cocktail, then we'll learn each other's names over pancakes in the morning, and after that, maybe, we can think about venturing into international waters together.

DEREK: Let's spend a lifetime together never knowing each other's names. Let's get new names!

LINDA: New names, new passports — is all that necessary to open a record store in Brazil?

DEREK: How long are we staying in Brazil?

LINDA: I don't know. How long do people who run away together stay... ran away?

DEREK: I've never run away with anyone before.

LINDA: Me neither. They do it all the time in movies.

DEREK: Even with the wrong footwear?

LINDA: They never say.

DEREK: Huh.

LINDA: Yeah, hmm.

DEREK: Are you staying here in the hotel?

LINDA: I've got a room.

DEREK: Is it occupied by... you know?

LINDA: No. My genetic colleagues have retreated to another part of the hotel. Are you inviting yourself up?

DEREK: I don't know what I'm doing.

DEREK and LINDA sip their drinks quietly.

LINDA: Um. Forgive my asking — as a former — what was it?

DEREK: Field directives—

LINDA: Right! As a former field directives liaison for an "underground redistribution syndicate", is it necessary for you to leave the country immediately?

DEREK: No. No, it's nothing like that.

LINDA: Okay.

DEREK: I was supposed to help stop the release of this really awful phone app that collects and logs every thought in your head.

LINDA: What's wrong with that? Sounds neat. You'd never lose a brilliant idea in the shower again. You could look back on those weird dreams where you're grocery shopping and all of sudden you run over your mother with a car and then you're taking an algebra test naked in a lion cage.

DEREK: What if you could be imprisoned for dreaming about murdering your mother because the government decided that unconsciously thinking about something is as bad as actually doing it?

LINDA: Oh, no, that's terrifying.

DEREK: Yeah.

LINDA: But you didn't create the app, right?

DEREK: No. It's just — this was my chance to do good, you know? After years of scamming and swindling, I could say we pulled a job that was for a greater purpose than self-enrichment. I had one small task and I blew it big time.

LINDA: Okay, but regardless of whether this app reaches people, there's gotta be, like, half a dozen ones in development right now. Soon, the market will be flooded with thought-logging apps, copycats and knock-offs, all with their little proprietary modifications and slightly different methods of tracking. Who knows which one will be more accurate? Eventually, it'll all be considered useless bullshit because the science behind it was junk anyway.

DEREK: Are you telling me not to quit my con job?

LINDA: No. Quit, if that's what you want. I wish I were brave enough to make such a substantial life decision.

DEREK: There's always our Brazilian record store.

LINDA: We don't know anything about each other. We're nameless strangers in a bar who don't know whether the other one snores or picks their nose or has a secret family in Wapakoneta or hates potatoes.

DEREK: We could be together for twenty years and still not know any of that.

LINDA: Hmpf.

DEREK: You don't want to leave your family?

LINDA: They wouldn't notice if I left. I told them I was going for ice two hours ago — no text, no call, no uniformed messenger boy dispatched with murmurs of concern.

DEREK: You think they wouldn't notice if you didn't turn up tomorrow morning?

LINDA: *This* morning, my mother told me that she had cancer. She had cancer for a year. She went through the diagnosis, treatments, everything — all without telling me. Told my sister, not me. She was there, not me.

DEREK: Jesus.

LINDA: And, now, Mom's apparently fine. Three weeks ago, I get a call from her asking if we can have a vacation in Orlando. I thought, okay, sure, it might be fun to be on vacation with my mother as adults.
You know what's not fun is learning about a parent's near-death experience over a continental breakfast surrounded by other families in their matching t-shirts and toddlers dressed as cartoon princesses and so many goddamned Spider-men. So, would they notice? Would they care? Would it feed some narrative they've constructed about me always abandoning them because I moved out of our shitty racist hometown the first chance I got? I don't know. Maybe I shouldn't care anymore.

DEREK: I'm sorry.

LINDA: *I'm* sorry. I need another drink.

LINDA signals for the bartender to bring another drink. DEREK does the same.

LINDA: Okay, we'll let fate decide.

DEREK: Decide what?

LINDA: The rest of our life.

DEREK: You wanna flip a coin?

LINDA: No. Better than that — let's say, if the next person who walks through that door is dressed as a unicorn, we agree to just spend the night together. If a panda and a wizard enter together, we'll… go to Tampa for the rest of the weekend. And, if —

DEREK: Wait, why would a panda and a lizard be hanging out together?

LINDA: Wizard, not lizard.

DEREK: Alright, why would a panda and a wizard be hanging out together?

LINDA: Somewhere, in some animated universe, there's probably a wizard and a panda who are best friends and have adventures.

DEREK: Gotcha. Go on.

LINDA: Right… if the pianist comes back first and plays anything other than "The Girl from Ipanema", we'll spend the rest of our lives together, for better or worse. But if Sam plays it again, we shake hands and part ways forever.

DEREK: Alright… what if the actual girl from Ipanema walks in?

LINDA: You can try your luck with her.

DEREK: Anything's possible. A lot of weird stuff going on in this hotel, yeah?

LINDA: There's a lot of weird stuff going on in this city.

DEREK: Maybe we belong here.

LINDA: You calling me weird? What happened to all the "you look normal" stuff from earlier? Was that just a pick-up line?

DEREK: It isn't. I mean, you're not. No. It's just — you're not made up like a tourist or a pirate, princess, whatever. But you're not normal — you're so wonderfully abnormal.

LINDA: You are an absolute nut and I'm pretty sure you're going to murder me.

DEREK: Ooh! She's back, the pianist.

LINDA and DEREK clasp hands, bracing for the impending chords. A piano version of "One Note Samba" begins.

LINDA: Well.

DEREK: That's… different.

LINDA: If it doesn't work out, we can blame it on the bossa nova.

DEREK: Where's the bartender? We need champagne.

LINDA: Let's go. We'll have room service send up a bottle.

DEREK and LINDA get up.

DEREK: With shrimp cocktail. And popcorn!

LINDA: And fuzzy slippers.

DEREK: And an atlas.

LINDA grabs a bar napkin.

LINDA: We're gonna forget all this. Let's write it down. You got a pen?

DEREK: *(pats his jacket and jeans pockets)* Er. I think I lost it in the elevator. Let's just ask the front desk.

DEREK and LINDA exit the bar.

END OF SCENE. BLACK OUT.

About Katharine!

Katharine is the author of the best-selling *30 Failures by Age 30, The Curable Romantic: Advice for the Romance-Impaired, Slantindicular: Stories Among Other Things* and the author-illustrator of *BORIS: Robot of Leisure.*

Katharine is also an artist and graphic designer specializing in low-brow pop art inspired by 20th century popular culture. Katharine's paintings, part of her Robot of Leisure series, have been exhibited in galleries and public spaces across North America. View more of her work at thatkatharine.com.

www.ingramcontent.com/pod-product-compliance
Lightning Source LLC
Chambersburg PA
CBHW050441010526
44118CB00013B/1630